# British Rail Sl
# The Final Years

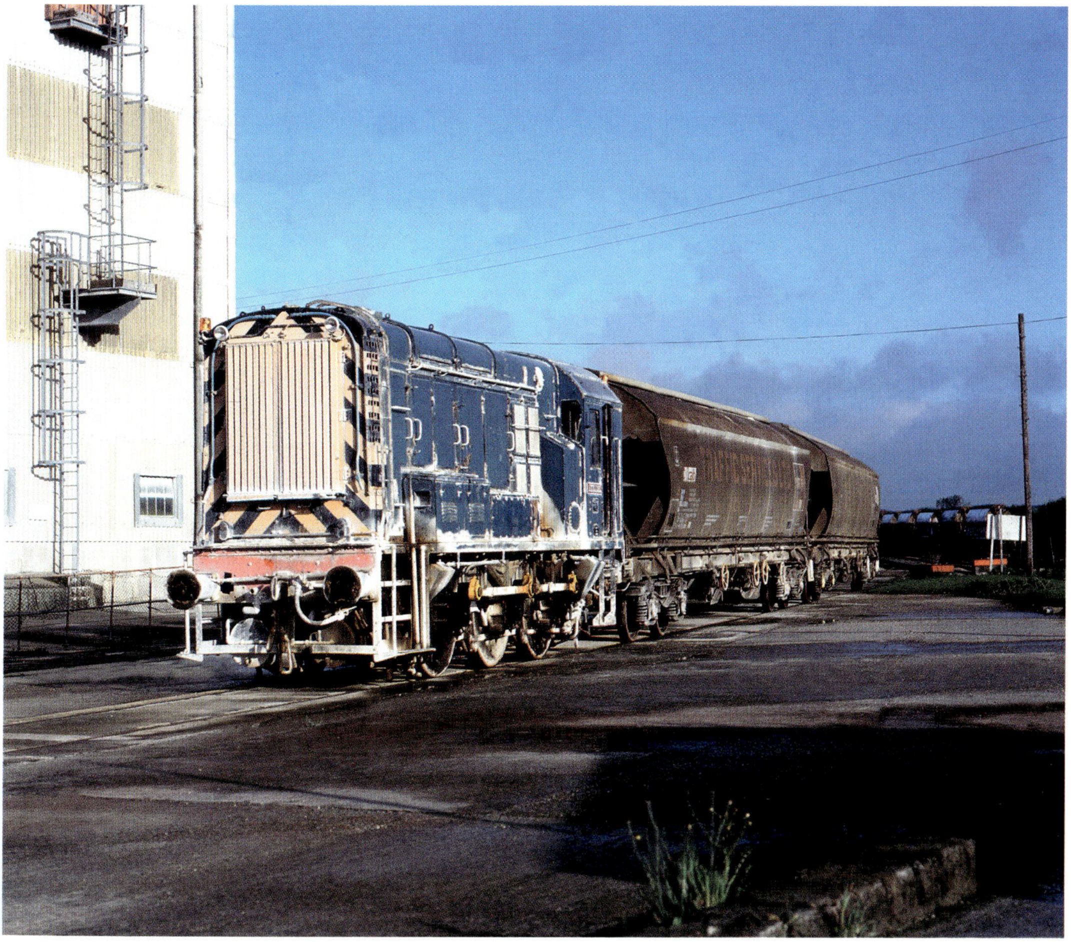

SIMON BENDALL

KEY Books

BRITAIN'S RAILWAYS SERIES, VOLUME 52

**Front cover image**: The end of the restricted-height Burry Port and Gwendraeth Valley branch was at Cwmmawr, where cut-down cab 08995 *Kidwelly* is seen marshalling empty HEA coal hoppers in October 1992. Carrying Railfreight Coal colours, it would later trundle back to Coedbach with the set of wagons in the process of being loaded alongside.

**Title page image**: Ex-BR shunters could still be found in industrial use during the 1990s, although their numbers were in decline as closures took effect, with many locos finding their way into preservation. In superb evening light, English China Clays-owned Class 08 P402D *Annabel*, better known as 08398, shunts two JIA Polybulks at Rock Dries on 27 May 1993. In railway parlance, the location is Goonbarrow Junction on the Newquay branch, which can be seen in the background along with a rake of stabled Clay Tigers. This expansive site still dispatches clay by rail today, but the shunter is long gone. Acquired in 1986, 08398 was sent for scrap in September 2010 after a period out of use, being replaced by an industrial.

**Contents page image**: Nine Class 08s received the red and grey colours of Rail Express Systems between 1991 and 1996, the majority being done towards the end of this period. While some were repainted at Crewe Works, others were done by their home depots, including 08714 at Cambridge in May 1994. Three months later, it was still looking resplendent on the depot's fuel point on 6 August. It was named *Cambridge* eight weeks later to mark the 25th anniversary of the Cambridge Railway Circle.

**Back cover image**: One of the highlights for the Class 08 fleet in 1992–93 was the modification of a dozen locos with altered gearing to create additional Class 09s, these having an increased top speed to allow use on trip workings. Previously 08759, a sparkling 09106 had only recently emerged from the RFS workshops at Kilnhurst when pictured at Thornaby in August 1993.

Published by Key Books
An imprint of Key Publishing Ltd
PO Box 100
Stamford
Lincs PE9 1XQ

www.keypublishing.com

The right of Simon Bendall to be identified as the author of this book has been asserted in accordance with the Copyright, Designs and Patents Act 1988 Sections 77 and 78.

Copyright © Simon Bendall, 2023

ISBN 978 1 80282 586 2

All rights reserved. Reproduction in whole or in part in any form whatsoever or by any means is strictly prohibited without the prior permission of the Publisher.

Typeset by SJmagic DESIGN SERVICES, India.

# Contents

**Introduction** ..................................................................................................................................4
**Chapter 1**    Southern Region ........................................................................................6
**Chapter 2**    Western Region .......................................................................................16
**Chapter 3**    Midland Region .......................................................................................39
**Chapter 4**    Eastern Region ........................................................................................62
**Chapter 5**    Anglia Region .........................................................................................83
**Chapter 6**    Scottish Region .......................................................................................90

# Introduction

As the 1990s dawned, the variety once found in British Rail's shunter fleet was all but gone. The early years of the previous decade had seen the last pair of Class 01s withdrawn along with the sole remaining Class 05 and the last few Class 06s, while the demise of Tinsley Yard had taken the two surviving Class 13s with it in January 1985. Even the Class 03s were extinct in service on the mainland with just two stragglers remaining in use on the Isle of Wight, along with a few withdrawn examples still awaiting disposal. The departmental Class 97/6s were little better, with just three of the original five machines in operation.

It therefore fell to the Class 08s and their faster Class 09 sisters to fly the shunter flag as British Rail entered its last few years of existence. While a far cry from the previous decade, the Class 08 fleet strength was still reasonably healthy in January 1990 with just under 450 examples operational, while more than 50 others were condemned and awaiting disposal across the country. The Class 09s were still at full strength with 26 examples available, although official totals showed just 25, on account of the allocation of 09017 to departmental stock as the Severn Tunnel emergency train loco 97806.

While there may have been a lack of variety in shunter types, there was no shortage of colour as the kaleidoscope of liveries that had emerged during the latter half of the 1980s continued to expand. The long-standing dominance of BR Corporate blue was under increasing threat as Departmental grey emerged as the livery of choice for shunters passing through BR workshops for major overhauls. Fortunately, the drabness of the official colour scheme was alleviated by numerous depots, which still found ways to customise their charges with special repaints or adornments.

However, the ever-decreasing levels of freight traffic, coupled with further modernisation and the need to reduce costs due to cuts in government subsidies, ensured that the shunter fleet total was only ever going in one direction; downwards. The closure of the Speedlink wagonload network in July 1991 brought the loss of trip workings and yard duties that hit the Class 08s hard, with numerous locos simply switched off as surplus to requirements. There was also a concerted effort to withdraw the members of the class that were still vacuum braked-only, as these were an inconvenience on an increasingly air-braked network.

On the passenger side, the switch of InterCity services to fixed-formation push-pull operation on both the West Coast Main Line and Great Eastern further impacted the need for station pilots, while the introduction of additional new Diesel Multiple Units (DMUs) by Regional Railways had a similar effect. Overnight mail work still provided gainful employment at large stations, but even this was under threat as unremunerative routes were systemically cut.

In the run-up to privatisation, the shunter fleet underwent considerable restructuring along with the rest of the motive power roster during 1994 as locos were divided amongst new business units, bringing yet more liveries, as they were prepared for sale over the following three years. This book takes a look at the many developments that took place over these final years of British Rail's existence, taking 1996 as its cut-off as this year saw most of the Class 08s and Class 09s pass into private ownership. As in the first volume, this is done on a region-by-region basis to give structure to the photos.

One Class 08 that was difficult to miss, and intentionally so, was 08715, which was repainted in Day-Glo orange at Stratford in October 1993. This was an experiment to improve the visibility of shunters working at night in Freightliner terminals and included the fitting of additional lights. However, as the last operational vacuum braked-only member of the class, it was of limited use and largely remained at the East London depot, where it is pictured on 19 March 1994. Under EWS ownership, it would find a use at Carlisle Currock wagon repair depot, from where it was sent for scrap to T. J. Thomson's Stockton yard in February 2009.

The early 1990s saw shunter activity at main stations become increasingly nocturnal, largely to cater for marshalling mail trains. However, at Carlisle, there was still sleeper and Motorail activity to observe as well. On 29 September 1993, 08910 waits to shunt a sleeper portion onto a southbound working from Scotland.

# Chapter 1
# Southern Region

As 1990 began, the Class 08s and Class 09s found on the erstwhile Southern Region were still largely split between the depots of Ashford Chart Leacon, Selhurst and Eastleigh. The only exception was 09007, which was officially allocated to Stewarts Lane for the first half of the year, while 03079 and 03179 were still exiled on the Isle of Wight. However, the Class 09s were no longer confined solely to the region as 1989 had seen 09001 and 09015 move to Cardiff Canton for use on steel traffic trip workings, while 09008 and 09013 had transferred to South Yorkshire for similar duties, being based at Tinsley. Next to leave in 1991 were 09005 and 09014, both heading to Knottingley for use by Railfreight Coal.

Those allocated to Chart Leacon and Selhurst were assigned to the departmental fleet and were typically found at the yards handling engineers' traffic, including Ashford pre-assembly depot, Tonbridge West Yard, Hither Green, Hoo Junction, Horsham and Three Bridges. In contrast, Eastleigh's allocation was sponsored by the Railfreight sector for a time, as its shunters were dispatched to the Freightliner terminal at Southampton Maritime and the nearby yard at Bevois Park, as well as the Hamworthy branch in Poole. Across the southeast, station pilot duties were now largely eradicated, but Bournemouth and Brighton both still had enough work to justify the provision of a shunter.

Significant changes took place during 1992 as the various departmental fleets were abolished and the locos divided up amongst the passenger sectors, with Network SouthEast given control of everything south of the River Thames. As a result, the Ashford shunter allocation was folded into that of Selhurst, while all of Eastleigh's Class 09s also followed, leaving just a small number of Class 08s based at the Hampshire depot.

Further restructuring took place in March 1994 in preparation for privatisation, with the newly created Trainload Freight South East operation, later to become Mainline Freight, allocated most of the Class 08s and Class 09s still based at Selhurst and Eastleigh. There were exceptions, though, with 09004/25/26 assigned to the South Central train operating unit for use at Selhurst and Brighton, while the Ryde Class 03s were similarly handed over to the Island Line operation.

Railfreight Distribution ceased to use Class 33/2s to shunt the Dover train ferry during the autumn of 1993, Class 08s returning to handle loading and unloading operations until the service ended in December 1995 following the opening of the Channel Tunnel. On 7 July 1995, 08913 and 08837 were operating in tandem at Dover Western Docks, both being out-based far from their home depot of Tinsley.

By the time it was pictured in March 1992, 08796 had been withdrawn for nearly two years at Chart Leacon. This had transferred to Ashford in September 1989 after almost three decades spent on the Western Region, but was condemned within a few months of its arrival due to its poor condition. Disposal would take place in April 1993 at the Glasgow yard of MC Metals, where so many of the class would end up in the early 1990s.

Although finished in Railfreight triple grey, 08950 was part of Ashford's departmental allocation when recorded at Tonbridge West Yard on 21 April 1991. The colours had been applied at Crewe Works during overhaul in May 1989 and amply illustrates why the switch to using Departmental grey for shunters was made soon after its completion. On this day, it was keeping company with 73105 and 47330.

A dozen of the original Class 09/0 shunters received Departmental grey during works attention between 1990–92, including 09011, which was released from Crewe Works following overhaul in January 1991. By 8 September that year, the Ashford-based loco was on duty at Tonbridge West Yard. It would survive for another 20 years under Railfreight Distribution and EWS ownership, being scrapped in November 2011.

Under Mainline Freight ownership, 09003 was treated to some livery embellishments, gaining a black roof, red solebars and silver numbers but with the shade of blue remaining resolutely BR rather than Mainline. By October 1996, it was stationed at Hither Green, complete with 73C shedplates on the battery box covers. Now based at Stewarts Lane after leaving Selhurst, it was part of the EWS fleet.

The Sheerness Steel works on the Isle of Sheppey made use of two Class 08s acquired from British Rail throughout the 1980s and on into the early 1990s. By January 1991, 08133 had notched up almost a decade of industrial service as it marshals the company's own fleet of JXA scrap wagons. The smart blue and red livery had been applied around a year earlier, with sale into preservation coming in 1995. This was initially at the South Yorkshire Railway but today the loco is based at the Severn Valley Railway.

From 1992 and with the plant now owned by Co-Steel, hired-in shunters began to appear at Sheerness as age caught up with 08133 and its partner 08216. This included Class 08s provided by RFS Industries, with 08596 recorded on site on 28 August 1994. This was 006 in RFS' number series, while the 'Loco No. 19' is left over from its time hired to the Channel Tunnel Trackwork Group (CTTG) for use on construction trains at Cheriton.

With the restructuring of the shunter fleet for privatisation, a number of locos were assigned to the newly created train operating units to support their passenger operations, invariably as depot pilots. 09004 was one of three Class 09s to be allocated to South Central, later coming under Connex control. The loco was stabled at Norwood Junction on 28 May 1995, but later fell out of use and would be sold for preservation five years later.

Three Class 09s received official names while based on the Southern, 09012 becoming *Dick Hardy* in April 1988 at the same time as it gained InterCity Executive colours. However, October 1990 saw it return from an overhaul at Crewe, repainted in Departmental grey and with the nameplates removed in error. While they would later be re-fitted, the nameless shunter is seen at Stewarts Lane on 3 February 1991, with 33206.

By June 1994, 08600 was an anonymous member of the Trainload Freight South East fleet based at Eastleigh, its days as Slade Green pilot under the guise of 97800 *Ivor* having come to an end at the beginning of the decade. Its Network SouthEast livery would follow in the spring of 1991 upon overhaul at Crewe. Today, it is owned by AV Dawson and based at its Middlesbrough terminal.

09025 was part of Eastleigh's allocation for 13 years between 1979 and 1992, the second half of this period seeing it carry the unofficial name of *Victory* along with Network SouthEast logos. During June 1992, it was recorded shunting YCV Turbots alongside Eastleigh station, just five months before transfer to Selhurst. The shunter also became part of the South Central fleet, going on to receive Connex yellow and white in 1998.

With a portable headlight in place, Mainline Freight's 08854 stands at the south end of Eastleigh depot in February 1996, with the carriage washer in the background. The shunter had just tripped a selection of engineers' wagons, including two Salmon flats and a Gunnell ballast hopper, from the East Yard, using the depot loop that still runs from the Portsmouth line around the rear of the adjacent works.

One short-lived livery oddball was 08933, which gained two Day-Glo orange stripes on its cabsides in October 1990 upon its return from overhaul at Crewe and repaint into Departmental grey. The reason for this has never been established, but they may have been connected to the shunter's appearance in a TV commercial for beer around this time. Pictured at Eastleigh that month, the loco did briefly work at Woking in this condition.

July 1993 saw 08649 repainted back into BR green at Eastleigh, gaining the depot's Spitfire depot plaques as well as the name *G. H. Stratton*. The following March saw it, along with 08847, officially transferred to the works, ensuring that shunters were included as part of the sale of the site into private ownership. During August 1994, the green machine awaits its next duty alongside a collision-damaged 4-VEP.

With Eastleigh Works subsequently coming under the control of Wessex Traincare Ltd, 08649 swapped its understated BR green for this complex scheme in 1996, the grey base being adorned with red, white and blue elements and WTL lettering. The nameplates and depot plaques were retained along with its original D3816 identity, the shortened number of '649' only appearing on the bufferbeams, as seen that September.

An earlier but subsequently displaced Eastleigh Works pilot was 08642, which gained its lined London and South Western Railway black livery in June 1989. When pictured in the evening sun on 4 September 1993, it was on hand at Southampton Maritime and in Network SouthEast ownership. Six months later, it would pass to Railfreight Distribution control and then Freightliner, going for scrap in 2006 still in the livery.

Also from the Eastleigh allocation, 09026 *William Pearson* was based at Salisbury for part of 1992 to assist with track-laying operations at the new maintenance depot for the soon to be introduced Waterloo−Exeter Class 159 DMUs. Pictured on 10 September, it displays the Crewe Works version of Departmental grey with a black cab door and upper bodywork. It would later become the third Class 09 to pass to Connex control.

Both of the Class 03s based on the Isle of Wight survived into the early 1990s, but with ever-decreasing use. During July 1990, 03079 was stabled in the engineers' sidings at Sandown, awaiting its next duty. This was the longer-lived of the duo in use on the island, its official withdrawal coming in June 1996, by when it was part of the Island Line train operating unit. Preservation at the Derwent Valley Railway would follow.

Network SouthEast-liveried 03179 was also to be found at Sandown on the same day in June 1990. Although it did not arrive at Ryde until 1988, it was the first of the pair to be condemned, this coming in October 1993. However, after five years in store, it would be surprisingly reprieved, with sale to West Anglia Great Northern and transfer to Hornsey depot in North London. Preservation would eventually come in 2016.

# Chapter 2
# Western Region

Old Oak Common still boasted a sizeable Class 08 allocation in 1990, with the fleet strength hovering around the 18 mark. The ownership was initially split between Network SouthEast and Railfreight (although later combined under Railfreight Distribution), with shunters dispatched to Paddington and Marylebone as well as Southall Yard and the coal concentration depot at West Drayton, while others worked locally at Old Oak Common, including at the HST depot and carriage sidings. Reading also still maintained a small allocation to cover the station and yards while others were sent to Didcot and Oxford. In addition, one of the Class 97/6s was normally present in the engineers' sidings at Reading.

Heading west, the next depot retaining an allocation of Class 08s was Bath Road, these working locally around Bristol, including at Temple Meads, St Philip's Marsh HST depot, Bristol East engineers' sidings and on trips to Avonmouth and Stoke Gifford. Despite the varied duties, all were assigned to the Railfreight sector.

Laira's entire allocation was initially the responsibility of InterCity as the decade began but soon moved to Railfreight, with Class 08s sent eastwards to Exeter, Taunton concrete works and Meldon Quarry. In Cornwall, Laira machines could be found at Penzance, St Blazey and, when hired to English China Clays, at Fowey Docks. Local duties around Plymouth included the station and covering the yards at Friary and Tavistock Junction.

Gloucester Horton Road began the decade with a trio of Class 08s based there, but these were merged into Cardiff Canton's allocation from July 1991, after which Gloucester became a duty for a single out-based shunter. This only increased the reach of the Welsh depot, where just over 20 Class 08s and Class 09s were provided to cover an area that stretched from Swindon, Westbury and Worcester to Barry. Around the Welsh capital, shunter locations included the yards at Tidal and Radyr along with a station pilot at Cardiff Central, while a quartet of machines was typically at work around Newport. Cardiff was also home to the remaining Class 97/6s, with one usually at Radyr and the other either spare at Canton or working at the carriage and wagon works at Cathays.

The sharp decline in the Welsh coal industry was reflected in a much reduced workload for the Landore fleet, although a total of ten or so Class 08s was still initially maintained. This included the trio of cut-down cab Class 08/9s to work over the Burry Port and Gwendraeth Valley line to Cwmmawr, although only one example was required on duty at a time. Other locations that required a pilot included Maliphant carriage sidings and Burrows Yard in Swansea, and a trio out-based at Margam.

The preparations for privatisation brought substantial restructuring in March 1994, with the creation of the regional freight companies. At the London end of the Great Western Main Line, Trainload Freight South East took over both the Reading and Old Oak Common allocations, concentrating them at the latter. Meanwhile, the Canton fleet passed to Trainload Freight West, later Transrail, this including the trio of Class 08/9s transferred across from Landore along with Severn Tunnel loco 97806. The freight operator also took part of the Laira allocation and transferred their maintenance to St Blazey.

The Class 08s that remained at Bath Road, Laira and Landore passed to the Great Western train operating unit at the same time, the Bristol allocation moving the short distance to St Philip's Marsh when Bath Road was closed in 1995. Lastly, the Cardiff Valleys operation was assigned 08830 for use at Canton.

One of the most high profile roles undertaken by a Class 97/6 occurred in late 1992 and early 1993 when 97654 was employed on works trains as part of the remodelling of the approach to Paddington, this project taking place while the station remained partially operational. During November 1992, the Ruston-built loco was recorded with a Satlink-liveried Queen Mary bogie brake van converted to a personnel carrier.

Old Oak Common retained a shunter allocation throughout the 1990s, even as it passed through the ownership of Network SouthEast, Mainline Freight and EWS. On 17–18 August 1991, an open weekend was held at the depot, with 08634 being one of the exhibits outside the running shed. The '90' lettering on the battery box may well be a reminder to maintenance staff that it was one of the class fitted with 90-volt electrical systems, 110-volt being standard on later batches.

As a major maintenance facility, Old Oak Common tended to accumulate a number of withdrawn locos that acted as a source of spares. By June 1990, 08640 had been extensively cannibalised for parts as it awaits its fate outside the Factory in the company of 08887. The shunter had been withdrawn in November 1988 after suffering extensive collision damage to the other side of the cab, leaving it stoved in.

To increase the number of Class 09s available for trip workings, 1992–93 saw 12 Class 08s re-geared and overhauled by RFS at its Kilnhurst workshops in South Yorkshire. Those with 110-volt electrics were renumbered as Class 09/1s, while Class 09/2 covered those with 90-volt systems. First to be completed in July 1992 was 09101, formerly 08833, which was recorded at Old Oak Common on 14 July 1994. Now under Trainload Freight South East ownership, it had arrived from Reading four months earlier.

The two Class 08s based at the Park Royal plant of Guinness made occasional trips to Old Oak Common for maintenance, with 08060 *Unicorn* recorded on one such visit on 8 May 1990. With traction motors littering the foreground, the shunter makes an unlikely companion for a HST power car inside the legendary Factory.

With an age difference of nine years, Guinness-owned 08022 *Lion* and BR's 08944 illustrate the evolution of the Class 08 design during the Old Oak Common open weekend on 18 August 1991. Built in 1953 and withdrawn from BR service in 1985, vacuum-braked 08022 has the original strap-hinged bonnet doors and wooden cab doors while 08944, dating from 1962, features the later pressed bonnet doors, steel cab doors and dual brakes with the associated air compressor cabinet in front of the fuel tank.

Only six shunters received the attractive Mainline Freight blue livery, four of them being painted at Old Oak Common between August and October 1995. 08523 was the sole Class 08 and this is pictured on one of the turntable roads at the depot on 5 November 1996 in the company of 09018, with both now in EWS ownership. The other shunters painted at the 'Oak' were 09006/07, with 09019/24 done at Stewarts Lane.

Also now in EWS ownership, 08646 was another shunter captured residing around Old Oak Common's most famous feature in October 1996. This was based on the region for much of its life, arriving in West London in March 1994 upon the creation of the regional freight companies. The Railfreight livery had been applied in June 1989 at Crewe and was retained through to its ultimate demise at EMR's Kingsbury yard in November 2015.

Southall Yard was busy enough with engineers' trains to still warrant the provision of a shunter in the mid-1990s and, during June 1995, Mainline Freight's 08924 was on duty. This was another of the Reading allocation that had migrated to Old Oak Common the previous year, but was just over two years away from storage by EWS. Remarkably, it survived numerous years out of traffic and today works at Cardiff Tidal.

Dating from 1948, Class 11 12049 passed into the ownership of Day in 1972 following withdrawal, taking up residence at the company's aggregates terminal at Brentford in West London. Some 19 years later, it was recorded on site on 28 August 1991. It was donated to the Mid-Hants Railway seven years later, only to be severely damaged by a fire at Ropley shed in July 2010, leading to its disposal, again to EMR, Kingsbury.

Although only based on the Southern Region for less than two years in the mid-1970s, 08850 still acquired the trademark high-level brake pipes. During July 1990, it rumbles along the rear of Reading station with two Grampus ballast/spoil wagons in tow as Class 117 set L405 waits to rattle its way back to Paddington. 08850 would be withdrawn at the end of 1992 and today enjoys retirement on the North Yorkshire Moors Railway.

Mail traffic was still to be seen at Reading in the early 1990s as 08948 busies itself on 2 October 1992, marshalling a Mk.1 GUV and BG. The shunter would find some fame two years later when it became the depot pilot at the new Eurostar depot at North Pole, for which it was fitted with Scharfenberg couplings at Crewe Works. It still performs the same function across London at Temple Mills today but is little used.

Built in 1952, the first of the Class 97/6s was withdrawn in April 1987, beginning the subsequent decade stored alongside the Great Western Main Line at Reading. Carrying both 97650 and PWM650, the Ruston and Hornsby-built shunter is seen in this position on 13 March 1990. Of the five-strong class, it was the only one not to receive the all-over yellow Civil Engineers plant livery, instead retaining BR blue.

With Network SouthEast's Reading depot in the background, 97654 is seen in the adjacent engineers' yard on 26 August 1992, while shunting Salmon and Sturgeon rail carriers. With the preparations for privatisation, it initially passed to the ownership of Mainline Freight but was soon sold to one of the infrastructure companies, moving to Slateford Yard in Edinburgh early in 1997, from where it was eventually preserved.

08480 was a late addition to the ranks of green-liveried Class 08s, its transformation taking place at Old Oak Common in March 1994 just as Trainload Freight South East took charge. A year later, it was on duty at Didcot Yard on 3 April 1995, and carrying the unofficial name of *Blackbeard*. Didcot was always a good place to observe a shunter at work, as trains were often drawn alongside the station platforms.

From the Reading allocation, Railfreight Distribution-controlled 08507 rumbles along the up platform at Oxford in April 1992 with the name of *Alf* rather crudely applied. At this time, traffic in the university city typically justified the provision of two Class 08s from the Berkshire depot, these undertaking trip workings over the Morris Cowley branch as well as working in Hinksey Yard and pottering around the station environs.

Under Mainline Freight, the reach of Old Oak Common's shunters extended through to Swindon where 08460 is pictured on 8 September 1995. This had been repainted a year earlier into a light grey livery but retained the black cab window surrounds and dark grey roof associated with Departmental grey. Simply lettered 'TLF South East' in blue, it retained the unique look for a further 21 years.

One of the duties for the Swindon pilot was to trip scrap trains along the remains of the Highworth branch to the Cooper's Metals yard for loading. This branch also served the Rover automotive plant, which was still dispatching components by rail at this time. During June 1995, Mainline Freight's 08664 is seen alongside what is today the EMR scrapyard while 47338 *Warrington Yard* awaits departure from the Rover sidings.

Gloucester Horton Road would lose its remaining allocation of Class 08s from the summer of 1991, the city's remaining duty thereafter being resourced by Canton. Back in March 1990, Gloucester staff carried out repaints on 08778 and 08795, which both received Departmental grey but with small black numbers and with the cab door pillar also completely finished in black. 08778 displays its new look following completion.

On a misty morning in May 1990, Canton-allocated 08649 stands in the engineers' sidings at Gloucester with former Toad brake van DW17290, now converted to a personnel carrier. The loco is still in clean condition following an overhaul at Crewe Works the previous October, but was two months away from a transfer to Ashford Chart Leacon, a move that would ultimately lead to it becoming the Eastleigh Works pilot.

The open day at the two Bristol depots of Bath Road and St Philip's Marsh on 29 June 1991 provided the opportunity to photograph 08483 and 08897 on Bath Road's fuel tank road. 08483 had been overhauled at Kilnhurst three months earlier, while the much dirtier 08897 was completed at Crewe in November 1989, allowing the different treatments of the black window surround to be compared. Creeping into shot, 47704 now belonged to the Parcels sector after displacement from ScotRail duties by the new Class 158s.

As a frontline InterCity depot, Bath Road had a tendency to splash the paint around, repainting a number of Class 47s and HST power cars. A more unlikely recipient was 08800, which became the only member of the class to receive full InterCity Swallow garb in May 1990, despite being Railfreight owned! Pictured on 3 April 1991, it was an early withdrawal in January 1993 and was scrapped 12 months later.

One of Bath Road's duties was to provide a shunter to the HST depot at St Philip's Marsh a short distance away, which on 16 April 1991 was being covered by 08410. Like other Class 08s assigned to HST depots, it is fitted with a buckeye coupling to give compatibility with the sets but on this occasion, it was attached to the unique HST generator coach 6310. This was converted from a Mk.1 BG over a decade earlier.

Bristol was a centre of mail operations for many years, with numerous parcels vans allocated to the city's depots for maintenance. Seen in the summer of 1996, 08819 *Steep Holm* was part of the Rail Express Systems fleet based at Crewe Diesel but out-stationed at Bristol Barton Hill. Painted at Crewe Works in May 1995, it was now EWS-owned and is seen shunting the stock from a Wales & West Weymouth working at Temple Meads. The matching BR brake van provided a safe riding platform for the groundstaff.

Foster Yeoman and its successor Mendip Rail has made use of second-hand Class 08s at Merehead Quarry since the mid-1970s and this continues today, albeit somewhat reduced as age takes its toll. Having passed to Yeoman ownership in 1975, 08032 was still going at the Somerset terminal on 27 June 1992, albeit battle-scarred. This had become No. 33 *Mendip* under the company's numbering system and was eventually retired to the Mid-Hants Railway in 2008.

Over the years, Yeoman and Mendip Rail has made the occasional additional Class 08 purchase, this typically allowing an older classmate to be stood down. Withdrawn in 1992, 08652 was acquired the following year and is seen outside the maintenance shed at Merehead on 23 June 1994. This became No. 66 in the Yeoman series, its smart appearance contrasting with 08032 (No. 33) alongside.

The restructuring of the shunter allocations in March 1994 brought several significant changes. For example, the Exeter locos switched from being provided by Laira to instead coming from the Canton allocation, with a number of Class 08s transferred to the Welsh depot as a result. Now assigned to the newly created Trainload Freight West, large-numbered 08801 was stabled at Exeter St Davids on 21 April 1994.

08645 has been based at Laira for almost 40 years now, having first arrived at the Plymouth depot in December 1983. However, in July 1990, the shunter was out of service with its centre wheelset removed, despite having only returned from overhaul at Crewe Works two months earlier. It became one of the Class 08s assigned to the Great Western train operating unit in 1994 and remains so today.

For much of the 1990s, commercial freight traffic operated over the Bodmin & Wenford Railway, this seeing VGA vans tripped to the rail-connected Fitzgerald Lighting factory at Bodmin for loading with electrical components. The vans would be deposited at Bodmin Parkway by the BR loco, and later by Transrail and EWS traction, and then tripped over the preserved line by the resident shunter, 08444. Withdrawn in November 1986, this had been restored to BR green as D3559 by 9 April 1990, as it departs from Parkway.

The early 1990s saw St Blazey shunters continue to be provided from the Laira allocation, this lasting until March 1994 when the Cornish depot regained an allocation upon the creation of Trainload Freight West. A long-term resident was 08955 *Peter*, which is pictured undergoing attention alongside a CDA clay hopper on 8 July 1991. Finished in BR blue, it carries a Railfreight Distribution repeater stripe by the cab door.

With the demise of the Class 10s owned by English China Clays at the end of the 1980s, a BR Class 08 was often hired in to work at Fowey Docks thereafter. On 9 April 1990, it was the turn of 08954 to marshal the CDA hoppers in the picturesque riverside location. The shunter had been overhauled at Crewe the previous summer, bringing the application of Railfreight triple grey, which would later gain a Transrail logo.

08644 had reached the limit of the Cornish rail network in the summer of 1995 as it stands in platform four at Penzance with the stock for the overnight Travelling Post Office. The welcome sign had been installed over a year earlier and was carved from granite. Finished in InterCity Mainline, 08644 had been painted for a second time at Laira in July 1991 but had recently lost its unofficial *Ponsandane* name from the fuel tanks.

97806 (ex-09017) was the first Class 09 to depart from the Southern in 1987 after it was selected to become the dedicated motive power for the Severn Tunnel emergency train. Although usually stationed at Sudbrook, the train was occasionally stabled at Newport if engineering work blocked its route. This was the case on 11 August 1994 as 97806 reposes on Godfrey Road. Now a Trainload Freight West asset, it would be returned to normal service as 09017 by EWS, with any available Class 09 instead provided to work the train.

Further Class 09s would move to South Wales in 1989 with the arrival of 09001 and 09015, while 09008 and 09013 followed in 1993 after a few years at Tinsley. Trip workings between Newport Alexandra Dock Junction and Llanwern formed part of their duties, with 09008 *Leona* recorded on Godfrey Road on 15 July 1994. The Canton depot plaques and Metals sub-sector repeaters added a certain something to the grey.

Cardiff Canton's shunter allocation was 21 strong on 28 June 1992, as 08804 and 08786 take a break on shed. The latter had only recently arrived in South Wales after a six-year spell at Thornaby and a stopover at RFS' Kilnhurst workshops for overhaul. In contrast, 08804 had spent much of the 1980s working off the depot, only broken by an 18-month stint at Old Oak Common before returning west.

The needs of the Allied Steel & Wire (ASW) plant at Tremorfa have long provided employment for Class 08s stationed at the adjacent yard of Cardiff Tidal. During 1996, Transrail-liveried 08955 stands amidst a selection of wagons, some of them only for internal use, awaiting its next job. Now owned by Celsa, the steelworks still employs Class 08s today, these being hired from GB Railfreight via a sub-contract with HNRC.

The transfer of the Class 08/9s from Landore to Canton in March 1994 greatly expanded their sphere of operation, although 08994 was out of use by this time with defects. With only one of 08993 and 08995 required to work to Cwmmawr, this left the other free to potter around Cardiff. On 3 May 1995, 08995 *Kidwelly* crosses Cargo Road while returning empty internal wagons from Queen Alexandra Dock to Tidal via a reversal at Channel Sidings. The wagons had earlier brought coiled wire from ASW for export.

The Cheltenham branch of the Railway Correspondence & Travel Society (RCTS) organised a brake van tour of the Cardiff docks internal system on 12 June 1996, for which Class 09 pioneer 09001 was provided as power. Seen during a photo stop at Splott, the loco had received a fresh coat of BR blue in June 1994 at Canton, although the BR arrows had recently been removed from the battery box covers.

Once described as the dirtiest place in Europe, the National Smokeless Fuels phurnacite plant at Abercwmboi, to the south east of Aberdare, closed in 1990 after decades of complaints about its polluting effects on the local area. With dismantling already underway, hired-in 08835 was on site in May 1990.

With so many Class 08s condemned in the late 1980s and early 1990s, it took some considerable effort to clear them from depots across the country in advance of privatisation. Many found their way to the Margam yard of Gwent Demolition, which involved road transfer to Port Talbot and then a short rail move. On 17 November 1993, Stratford's 08407 leads a doomed line-up of 08224, 08729, 08367 and 08420 at Port Talbot.

The height difference between 08994 *Gwendraeth* and 08895 is evident at Landore on 18 April 1992. 08895 would be withdrawn in September 1993, although it was another seven years before it was scrapped on site at Margam. 08994, meanwhile, was heading for a spell on the sidelines at Canton during 1994, but it would be repaired by Transrail the following year and resume work on the BPGV line ahead of its closure in 1996.

Withdrawn from Crewe in November 1986, 08598 was immediately sold into industrial use, moving to the PD Fuels coal preparation plant at Gwaun-Cae-Gurwen, to the north of Swansea, two months later. By October 1991, it had been repainted as it waits to shunt 21-ton coal hoppers relegated to internal use. It would later be sold to hire company RMS Locotec and today can be found at the Middlesbrough terminal of AV Dawson.

An earlier arrival at Gwaun-Cae-Gurwen in August 1984 was 08113, which had been withdrawn from Canton earlier in the year. By October 1991, it could be found stabled undercover and adorned with Powell Duffryn Coal Preparation (PDCP) logos. Also sold to RMS Locotec in 1995, it became a spares donor until scrapping in 2007.

PD Fuels made use of an ex-BR shunter at more of its sites in South Wales, with 07012 employed initially at Cwmmawr before moving to Coedbach. During October 1990, the former Southampton Docks shunter was to be found inside the small loco shed in the company of a fellow Ruston & Hornsby product, works no. 468048, dating from 1963. The Class 07 would be preserved during 1992 at the South Yorkshire Railway.

# Chapter 3
# Midland Region

With Cricklewood having closed in October 1988, Willesden was responsible for providing shunters at the London end of both the West Coast Main Line and Midland Main Line in the early 1990s. For the latter, this was a single Class 08 at both Cricklewood carriage sidings and St Pancras, while four were required in the Euston area. Otherwise, the yards around Wembley and Stonebridge Park still required six shunters.

Bletchley remained responsible for sending shunters to Rugby and Northampton as well as covering local requirements, including two at Wolverton Works. In the West Midlands, Bescot had become the sole provider of Class 08s from November 1988, with the absorption of the Tyseley fleet. Ten duties still existed across the conurbation, including at Birmingham New Street, Oxley and Tyseley. The yards at Bescot needed three Class 08s, with one each working at Bordesley, Washwood Heath and the steel terminals at Wolverhampton and Wednesbury.

On the Midland lines, Leicester no longer had an allocation of shunters so one was sent from Etches Park, with three others working around Derby and one out-based at the wagon shops at Burton. Illustrating the decline at Toton, three Class 08s were now sufficient to work the remaining yards, although another was assigned to Melton Mowbray for a time to cover the Charterail freight operation.

Crewe had suffered rather fewer cutbacks in its requirements, with nine shunters provided across the diesel and electric depots along with the works, station, carriage sidings and the yards at Basford Hall and Gresty Lane. In contrast, out-based duties were now limited to just Stoke, Chester and Holyhead. On Merseyside, Allerton was responsible for all shunters across the region and beyond early in the 1990s, its reach extending to Wigan Springs Branch, Ince Moss engineers' tip, Bolton, Preston and Warrington Arpley. More locally, duties still existed at Liverpool Lime Street, Garston Freightliner terminal and docks, Birkenhead North depot, Edge Hill carriage sidings and the yards at Dee Marsh, Ditton, Halewood and Ellesmere Port.

In Manchester, Piccadilly station still required a pilot from the Longsight allocation, with others working at the depot's carriage sidings along with the engineers' yards at Castleton and Guide Bridge and Trafford Park freight terminal. Finally, the Carlisle allocation could still be found around the station, along with Kingmoor Yard, Upperby carriage sidings and Currock wagon shops. The only remaining out-based turns were rather distant at Carnforth and Workington.

The March 1994 privatisation reorganisation brought significant alterations to the shunters across the region, where the number of duties had already considerably reduced. Trainload Freight West was given the Bletchley, Bescot and Carlisle allocations while it also took some of the Allerton fleet, which were transferred to Wigan Springs Branch. The rest of the Allerton shunters passed to Railfreight Distribution and now worked further afield, including some of the Crewe duties. Other Distribution shunters, including from the Tinsley allocation, were out-based at Wembley Yard and Saltley, the latter covering the likes of Washwood Heath and Bordesley.

The Toton shunters went to the future Mainline Freight while Rail Express Systems took most of the Crewe Diesel allocation with some working around the Euston area. Wolverton Works was given a pair of Class 08s while the Longsight and Willesden allocations went to the West Coast train operating unit. In the same way, the Midland TOU was assigned the Derby shunters, with two more returning to Tyseley for what would become Central Trains.

With the unofficial name of *Phil* painted on a bonnet door, 08648 rumbles around the throat of Euston station in September 1991. It was common to find a Class 08 on the west side of the terminus at this time, where it could shunt the Motorail stock and make trips to the Downside carriage sidings with mail vans. The loco had received Departmental grey exactly two years earlier at Crewe and was part of the Willesden allocation.

A short walk along Euston Road in the same period would typically reveal another member of the class at St Pancras, where its main employment was shuffling mail vans. In November 1991, another of the Willesden fleet was on duty as booked in the form of 08677. Despite the Network SouthEast branding on the battery box, it had spent part of the year allocated to InterCity before transferring to Railfreight control.

The privatisation process threw up some allocation anomalies for shunters. With Wembley Yard assigned to Railfreight Distribution control, shunters were drawn from the Allerton allocation as the company had no closer maintenance base to call its own. On 15 June 1996, 08389 *Saxon* was in residence in North London, this being a long-term Tinsley machine that had joined the Allerton fleet eight months earlier.

When BR's loco fleet was divided up between the regional freight companies in March 1994, Railfreight Distribution received a trio of Class 09s that had previously been based at Selhurst. Initially allocated to Tinsley, 09011/21/22 were soon reassigned to Allerton and at least one was often to be found at Wembley. On 28 April 1996, 09011 stands in the unfamiliar surroundings with the unofficial name of *Sudbury* applied.

Bletchley made a contribution to the ranks of Class 08s finished in 'heritage' liveries during April 1992 when 08519 was repainted in black with BR roundels, its original number of D3681 and the 'name' *Bletchley LMS*. On 9 October 1994, the shunter was stabled outside the depot building, notably being air-braked only following the removal of its vacuum pipes. Stored in 1996, it would be scrapped four years later.

08629 enjoyed a long association with Bletchley following its initial allocation to the depot in 1963, where it largely remained allocated for the next 31 years. For much of the sectorisation era, it could be found on the other side of Milton Keynes as works pilot at Wolverton, after which it was named. However, December 1992 saw it back at Bletchley and undergoing repairs.

August 1993 saw 08629 given a makeover at Wolverton to reflect its use at the home of the Royal train. The coat of claret ensured the shunter looked the part as it was often charged with shunting the prestigious coaches between their dedicated depot building and the exchange sidings on the West Coast Main Line. The repaint was completed in advance of a rare open day at the works, where it was pictured on 25 September.

Northampton was a longstanding shunter duty for a Bletchley Class 08 and on an unrecorded date in 1991, it was 08914 occupying the familiar spot in the north bays at the station. As well as marshalling parcels stock, it worked Castle Yard in the background, which was predominately used by engineers' stock at this time. It would be stored at Bescot in 1997 but scrapping would not take place until 2005.

Once the pride of Tyseley, the London Midland and Scottish black livery given to 08601 in October 1986 was looking somewhat tatty by the time it was recorded at Rugby on 8 October 1994. Now under Transrail ownership, it had become part of the Bescot fleet back in November 1988 and subsequently would also work at Northampton. Stored in 1999 at Allerton and then stripped for parts, the remains were cut up in 2005.

There was still sufficient work to require the presence of a Class 08 at Birmingham New Street in the early 1990s but the duty was coming to and. On 13 January 1991, 08924 had seen in the new year in the bowels of the station. The shunter had joined the Bescot allocation seven months earlier but was only passing through the West Midlands, as it would start 1992 allocated to Old Oak Common.

With the M6 motorway in the background, 08893 ticks over in Bescot Yard on 19 March 1993 as it awaits its next job. This was another Class 08 acquired by Bescot when Tyseley lost its allocation in November 1988, its previous Railfreight Red Stripe livery having been replaced by Departmental grey during overhaul at Crewe in June 1990. The open flap by the battery box gives access to the battery isolation switch.

Another refugee from Tyseley, 08805 forms the centre of a wintry scene at Bescot in January 1991 as it lies out of service with its coupling rods removed. The following month would see it hauled to Doncaster Works for repairs, including new wheelsets. In March 1994, it would become one of the pair of Class 08s selected to work for the Central train operating unit and it still performs this role in 2023 with West Midlands Railway. Currently based at Soho EMU depot, it still carries Railfreight Red Stripe, a fresh coat being applied in 2015.

A 22-year career based at Bescot had come to an end for 08901 as it lies withdrawn in the yard in the autumn of 1994. Stored the previous October, the shunter displays the hallmarks of its time stationed at Oxley carriage depot, Wolverhampton, with the paintwork stained white by the numerous trips through the carriage washer and its chemical wash. The rubber strips fitted along the solebar to provide rudimentary waterproofing to the springs and motion are still in place, these also featuring on 08765.

The infamous 08898 displays the catastrophic damage caused by sending a standard height Class 08 along the Burry Port and Gwendraeth Valley line on 9 November 1988. Instead of waiting at Coedbach for a failed Class 08/9 to be brought down so it could be hauled back to Landore, 08898 accompanied another of the reduced-height sub-class along the branch, coming a cropper on the first low bridge encountered. Seen in January 1991, the 'italic 08' awaits disposal at Bescot, which would finally come seven years later.

The launch of the innovative Pedigree Petfoods service between Melton Mowbray and Cricklewood required the provision of a shunter at the originating point to marshal the train of KOA 'piggyback' wagons as each one was loaded with a specialist Charterail road trailer. This was provided from the Toton allocation and on 18 October 1991, it was 08511 on duty in the former station yard. On occasions, a Class 20 was provided.

Having already illustrated the first of the Class 09/1 conversions, the doyen of the Class 09/2 fleet is seen at Toton on 28 December 1993. Previously 08421, 09201 was assigned to the Nottinghamshire depot upon completion of its modifications at RFS, Kilnhurst in October 1992 and would later pass to Mainline Freight ownership. Five '09/2s' would be created by the end of 1992, these having 90-volt electrical systems.

08597 and 08623 were enjoying a lazy Sunday in the sun on 6 September 1992 as they recline near the fuelling point at Toton. Both had moved to the Nottinghamshire depot in the middle of the previous decade, 08597 arriving from Etches Park in May 1984 while 08623 made the same journey in October 1985. The bank in the background has long provided an excellent vantage point over the depot and yards.

Following the creation of the Railfreight sub-sectors in October 1987, the colourful sector badges found their way onto several Class 08s, usually as an unofficial adornment. For example, 08829 had gained a Railfreight Coal logo meant for a HAA hopper when recorded at Toton on 2 January 1994. By this date, the loco's career was over, having been stored seven months earlier but it was 2005 before it was finally cut-up.

08602's BR career officially came to an end with withdrawal from Carlisle Kingmoor in March 1986. However, two years later, it was sold to RFS and moved to Doncaster, becoming 004 *Clarence* in the company's hire fleet. During 1991, it was sold again to ABB for use at Derby Litchurch Lane, where it is seen on 28 February 1994, having been repainted in green with its original number of D3769. It remained here until 2021.

With the creation of Trainload Freight West in March 1994, its share of the Allerton shunter fleet was transferred to Wigan Springs Branch for maintenance. On 15 June 1995, 08918 was some distance from its nominal home as it shunts aggregates hoppers at Dove Holes Quarry, Peak Forest. Now operating under the Transrail banner, Class 08s were by this time supplementing the resident industrial shunters.

Those shunters that remained based at Allerton from March 1994 were allocated to Railfreight Distribution with examples dispatched to Crewe to work in and around Basford Hall. On 4 May 1995, 08624 awaits the road at Crewe station as it hauls a Class 90 round to Crewe Electric for maintenance. Today, the loco forms part of the Freightliner fleet, being deployed to the company's container terminals across the country.

The allocation alterations of March 1994 saw the Class 08s based at Crewe Diesel come under the control of Rail Express Systems, of which 08742 was one. However, eight months earlier on 6 July 1993, it was notionally a Railfreight Distribution machine, although even then shunters still tended to be somewhat common-user. As a result, its use shunting parcels stock in Crewe station was not unusual.

Further illustrating this shared usage of shunters under BR, 08633 was a Railfreight Distribution loco when it received Rail Express Systems red and grey in October 1991 as one of the launch locos for the major rebrand of the Parcels sector. The same month saw the loco take part in an open day at Crewe Diesel, where it was named *The Sorter* on the 12th and is pictured following the unveiling ceremony.

Further Class 08s would eventually receive the Rail Express Systems colours but, in most cases, not until the sector had shunters to call its own. 08802 had been released from the nearby works just two months earlier following overhaul and repaint as the spotless loco rumbles through Crewe station in August 1995.

As with Derby, ABB made use of surplus Class 08s at Crewe Works following privatisation of the BR workshops. Withdrawn from Crewe Diesel in October 1993, 08699 was sold to ABB the following spring and moved the short distance to the works. By the time of the open day on 17 August 1996, it was anonymous in undercoat grey, which caused some confusion amongst enthusiasts at the time. Although the chalk markings on the battery box indicated it was made up of different locos, it was established that it was mostly 08699.

In June 1993, 08702 was occupying the spot usually reserved for the Chester area pilot when not in use, this being the parcels bays at the east end of the station. At this time, the main employment for the resident shunter was at the DMU depot and wagon repair shops, with Crewe Diesel supplying the loco from its allocation. 08702 would be stored by EWS five years later and scrapped by C. F. Booth, Rotherham, in 2004.

The eagle emblem applied to 08676's fuel tank marks the shunter out as once being part of Longsight's allocation, where it was based between 1984–94. However, when it was recorded at Ellesmere Port on 23 July 1995, it was assigned to Springs Branch and in Transrail ownership. The Merseyside yard remained an important freight hub at this time, with Shell's Stanlow refinery and numerous other terminals all nearby.

With a sizeable allocation of shunters, several could typically be found undergoing attention at Allerton, where maintenance space in the shed was shared with Freightliner container flats. On 16 February 1992, 08415 receives some engine repairs alongside three sister machines. The loco would be stored under Transrail ownership in November 1995, with disposal at EMR's Attercliffe yard coming two years later.

After 28 years based on the Western Region, including more than a decade at Bristol Bath Road, 08951 arrived on Merseyside in September 1990. By 24 January 1993, it was part of the Railfreight Distribution fleet and serving as depot pilot at Allerton, having gained Departmental grey in May 1990. The wagon in the background is a FBB two-axle container flat carrying a mobile office finished in Distribution red and yellow.

Allerton became quite infamous for the rows of cannibalised Class 08s that littered the depot in the early 1990s. On 15 October 1994, former Longsight favourite 08673 was already heavily stripped, having been withdrawn just five months earlier. Despite its condition, the shunter would linger at the depot until 2001 before being moved to Wigan Springs Branch. It was finally cut up at a Liverpool scrapyard in April 2003.

On a not so fine summer's day in August 1996, 08599 reposes on the stabling point at Warrington Arpley, quite possibly reflecting on its new life under EWS ownership. Prior to this, it had been part of the Rail Express Systems fleet and was still notionally based at Crewe Diesel at this time, although with the merging of the various companies acquired by the Wisconsin Central subsidiary, such allocations were rather moot.

Despite appearances to the contrary, this is not the 'italic 08' 08898 returned to full health but rather 08868 masquerading as its unfortunate sister at Baron Street sidings, Bury, on 23 July 1995. The shunter had been withdrawn in December 1992 and sold to Harry Needle, spending some three years at the East Lancashire Railway before commencing commercial hire work, initially at Conington tip, near Peterborough.

By 30 May 1994, 08611 had notched up a quarter of a century based at Longsight, but at this point in its career was stored out of use. It was now part of the West Coast train operating unit and would be returned to traffic in the summer of 1995, later coming under the control of Alstom to service its maintenance contract with Virgin Trains. It still works for Alstom today and was located at Wembley in the spring of 2023.

Newly repainted in BR blue, 08790 sparkles on shed at Longsight on 21 August 1994. The loco had survived a withdrawal attempt the previous year to also join the West Coast fleet, going on to gain the name *M. A. Smith* three months later. Its career subsequently followed that of 08611, joining the Alstom/Virgin fleet. While it has since worked at Wembley, Oxley and Edge Hill, it is now once again back at Longsight.

After six years of disuse, the Trafford Park estates railway in Manchester was returned to use during 1989. To provide motive power on the private system, two Class 08s were acquired from BR, including 08669. This was withdrawn from Longsight in March 1989 and immediately sold to the Trafford Park Railway Company, going on to acquire a green livery. It is seen stabled on the system on 30 May 1994.

The other Class 08 initially acquired was 08423, which was withdrawn from Springs Branch in November 1988 and again moved straight away to Trafford Park. Also repainted in green, the loco is seen at Longsight during 1990, having visited the depot to undergo tyre turning. With this completed, it stands outside the wheel lathe building with its coupling rods removed awaiting transfer back to Trafford Park.

Two more Class 08s, 08613 and 08615, would later be acquired for use at Trafford Park. Of these, 08615 was withdrawn and sold from Allerton in December 1993, making the move to Manchester two months later. When recorded on 30 May 1994, it was still in BR blue but with its arrows painted out. It would spend six years at Trafford Park before sale to Wabtec as part of its hire fleet. Today, it works at Shotton steelworks.

The Trafford Park estate was also home to a wheel foundry, which by the mid-1990s was under the ownership of ABB. Two overhauled Class 08s were provided to work the internal system in place of the previous industrial shunters, 08787 and 08943 becoming 001 and 002. In ex-works condition, 08787 is seen on 18 June 1995, six months after arrival. It was at this time that its identity became muddled with 08296.

Despite being at opposite ends of the Lake District, the Carnforth shunter duty was out-based from Carlisle Upperby. Newly added to the Trainload Freight West allocation, 08534 was on hand in the engineers' sidings on 1 April 1994, and complete with a Carlisle fox depot sticker on its cabside. It would be transferred to Motherwell the following summer and be scrapped at T. J. Thomson's Stockton yard in 2007.

In the days before modern safety systems were required, industrial shunters were occasionally authorised to travel over the BR network. Withdrawn in October 1988, 08678 was moved to Carlisle Upperby five months later for repairs and a repaint, having been sold to Glaxochem for use at its Ulverston plant. On 29 April 1989, the shunter stands in Plumpton loop, to the north of Penrith, part way through its delivery run to its new home. During November 1994 it was transferred to Carnforth and today works for West Coast Railways.

By 1994, the Steamtown centre at Carnforth was already turning towards commercial work and the operation of main line charter trains, a process that would see the site closed to the public after the 1997 season and the subsequent establishment of West Coast Railways. On 1 April 1994, Class 03 D2381 stands atop newly acquired Mk.1 buffet 1860 with the Pilkington 'K' set of Mk.1s in the background. D2381 was withdrawn in June 1972, never officially carrying its TOPS number, and is still at Carnforth in 2023.

Another distant outpost for a Carlisle Class 08 was Workington on the Cumbrian coast, where it worked the local yard and trip workings. At weekends, the shunter tended to stable at the station and during April 1992, 08690 was doing just this in the company of 60069 *Humphry Davy* and a Railfreight Coal Class 31. The '08' would move to Etches Park the following year, duly becoming part of the Midland Mainline fleet.

Previously pictured at Carnforth, 08534 is seen again but this time in June 1990 when it was newly ex-works from overhaul and repaint at Crewe, and with the depot plaque sticker already in place. The location is its home depot of Carlisle Upperby where it is shunting a Mk.2a TSO, two Mk.3a sleepers and a Mk.1 BG. In the background, Hunslet-Barclay's 20905 is stabled with the Schering Agrochemicals weedkiller set.

An interesting scene at Carlisle in the summer of 1994 as 08768 shunts two Motorail Mk.1 GUVs onto the rear of a southbound InterCity service to Euston. With such trains now using push-pull operation, the vans were added on top of the loco, in this case a Class 87, sandwiching it between the stock. Once coupled, the '08' would haul the side-loading ramp wagon away and stable in the holding sidings alongside the station wall.

# Chapter 4
# Eastern Region

At the start of the 1990s, Stratford was still supplying a Class 08 to act as station pilot at King's Cross, although the duty was withdrawn around mid-1993. Elsewhere in North London, shunters could still be found at Ferme Park and Bounds Green, the latter duty lasting until 2021. Further north, Hitchin and Peterborough both warranted shunters, these coming from the Cambridge and March allocations.

With Shirebrook no longer having a loco allocation, Class 08s for Worksop now came from Doncaster Carr, the rest of the depot's shunters otherwise working locally in the surrounding yards. Tinsley's much reduced fleet wandered slightly further afield, including to Rotherham steel terminal, Beighton permanent way yard and Sheffield station. One of the trip workings based at what was left of Tinsley Yard was specifically assigned to a Class 09 with 09008 and 09013 having moved north from the Southern Region in 1989, remaining until 1993.

In West Yorkshire, the area covered by Knottingley expanded significantly during 1990–91 as York relinquished its remaining Class 08s in two batches. Thereafter, Knottingley-allocated machines could be found at Hull and Goole along with Healey Mills, York and Crofton engineers' yard. In contrast, the Neville Hill Class 08s remained around Leeds, covering the depot and station along with Hunslet Yard and Stourton Freightliner terminal, the latter two duties working off Holbeck, which again no longer had its own allocation.

In Lincolnshire and on Humberside, the general downturn in freight traffic and use of privately-owned shunters meant that the Immingham Class 08s were now restricted to working around the local docks complex and at Scunthorpe. The needs of Tees Yard and the adjacent carriage and wagon workshops still occupied part of the Thornaby fleet, but, with a number of important freight terminals on Teesside, Class 08s could also be hired out when needed to ICI Wilton and the chemical works at Seal Sands.

Upon the closure of Gateshead in July 1991, the Class 08s that had remained based there transferred to the other side of the River Tyne and Heaton. As well as continuing to work at the carriage depot, a station pilot was still provided at Newcastle along with one shunter at each of Low Fell engineers' yard and Tyneside Central Freight Depot. Somewhat curiously, given the distances involved, the shunter for Sunderland South Dock still came from the Blyth Cambois allocation rather than Heaton's. Otherwise, Blyth's small allocation worked around the Northumberland depot, with the occasional hire to British Coal at Lynemouth Colliery, until the pool was abolished in November 1992.

With the commencement of the privatisation process in March 1994, Trainload Freight North East, soon to become Loadhaul, was assigned the shunters based at Doncaster, Knottingley, Immingham and Thornaby. Further south, Mainline Freight assumed responsibility for the shunters at Peterborough and Worksop, these now coming from Toton. Elsewhere, Railfreight Distribution took the Tinsley allocation while the Heaton Class 08s were placed with Rail Express Systems.

The two Stratford shunters based at Bounds Green at the time the fleet was divided up remained at the former InterCity depot as part of the East Coast fleet, while the same was true of those at Neville Hill, which were added to the Midland train operating unit. Finally, like other main workshops, Doncaster Works gained two pilots to call its own once again.

Built 28 years apart, 08821 keeps company with 91005 on the stabling sidings at King's Cross on 30 March 1991. Such a line-up was not uncommon at the London terminus early in the 1990s, with a spare Class 91 kept on hand while the new AC electrics were bedding in. With the full introduction of the push-pull Mk.4 formations, the need to provide a shunter all but disappeared, leading to the duty being withdrawn in 1993.

The first Class 08 to carry the triple grey Railfreight livery was 08834, which was re-liveried in preparation for the launch of the new sub-sector identities in October 1987. Also carrying Railfreight Distribution cabside markings, it was on duty at King's Cross in July 1992. Two months later, it would move to Cheriton for use on Channel Tunnel construction traffic as one of numerous BR Class 08s hired in for the project.

Despite its proximity to Yorkshire, freight activities at Worksop fell under the purview of what would become Mainline Freight rather than Loadhaul. As a result, it was Toton-based Class 08s that took up residence after the fleet reorganisation with TLF South East-branded 08441 recorded on duty on 5 June 1994. Having passed through EWS ownership to Railway Support Services, it would become the penultimate Class 08 to be based at Bounds Green, departing in March 2021 after the depot passed to Hitachi ownership.

With Lincoln being the centre of Ruston and Hornsby's manufacturing operations, the City of Lincoln Council opted to mark this industrial heritage by purchasing 97650 from British Rail in January 1990. Moved north the following month, it was placed on a short length of track outside the closed Lincoln Holmes shed, where it is seen on 1 April 1991. Initially re-homed in 1994, it now resides in the Heritage Shunters Trust collection.

An earlier acquisition by Lincoln Council in 1988 was 08102, which as D3167 was built at Derby Works in 1955. The end of 1988 saw it moved to Doncaster Works for a repaint into BR green, where it remained until the following spring when it was placed on display by Lincoln High Street signal box. The plinthed shunter is seen in its position alongside the BR lines on 22 June 1993.

Like 97650, 08102 was eventually released from its resting place at Lincoln, being lifted back onto BR metals on 8 May 1994, and hauled the short distance to Holmes Yard. The following day, the shunter is in the process of being winched aboard a low-loader for transfer to what is today known as the Lincolnshire Wolds Railway, where it still resides in operational condition. Road transport of shunters was still relatively unusual in 1994 but would become commonplace as privatisation took effect.

Now air-braked only, 08510 rests in the bay platform at Sheffield in April 1994 while Royal Mail staff load the three Mk.1 BGs behind. The loco had become part of the Tinsley allocation in February 1978, going on to gain the painted name of *Canklow* nine years later. The previous month had seen the loco become part of the newly created Trainload Freight North East fleet based at Doncaster, but it had yet to move to its new home.

When recorded at Beighton permanent way yard in 1993, 08879 *Earles* had been based around Sheffield for its entire life, joining the Tinsley allocation in April 1964 and where it remained for 34 years. As well as the painted name, Tinsley rose and shedplate, the shunter had gained the yellow chevrons used to denote a loco belonging to the Civil Engineers department, although they were purely for decorative effect in this case.

After 26 years based on the Southern Region, 09013 set out for pastures new in 1988, a year-long stay at Cardiff being followed by a four-year stint at Tinsley. The spotless shunter is seen on Tinsley depot on 21 July 1991, having just returned from overhaul at RFS, Kilnhurst, and a repaint into Departmental grey.

When pictured at Tinsley on 9 April 1994, 08389 *Saxon* was the second oldest Class 08 still in traffic, having notched up 36 years since acceptance in April 1958. Newly added to the Railfreight Distribution fleet, it was still going strong, unlike 08661 *Mercian* behind, which at this point in its career was stored unserviceable. However, by the autumn, it had been resurrected as RfD European-liveried *Europa* at Crewe Electric.

Loadhaul-owned 08512 was a visitor to Tinsley when recorded heading the familiar line of stabled shunters on 10 May 1995, alongside 08880. At this time, it was allocated to Doncaster Carr, having spent much of its career based in the northeast, including almost 25 years at Gateshead. The Railfreight colours had been applied in January 1989 while 47321, 37711 and 37095 are amongst the stabled main line traction.

Tinsley's latest creation enjoys the autumn sunshine as 08745 *The Tyke* reposes outside the depot in October 1994, following the completion of its repaint into the new Railfreight Distribution European scheme. Adapted from the similar Class 47 livery, this featured reproportioned grey bands and a dark blue roof. Although eight shunters would gain the livery, this was the only one done at Tinsley, the others being 08393/653/737 and 09021 at Allerton and 08751/946 at Saltley in addition to already mentioned 08661.

Tinsley's love of the paintbrush extended to customising numerous Class 08s, including returning 08691 to a version of green complete with *Escafeld* painted name in December 1989. In this form, it was often to be found on station pilot duties at Sheffield. By 5 March 1994, it was looking somewhat tatty as it spends the weekend at Tinsley. In 2023, the loco was still in use as part of the Freightliner fleet.

A new depot 'pet' was created by Tinsley in 1996, turquoise-liveried 08879 being unveiled at the depot's open day on 27 April when it was named *Sheffield Childrens Hospital*. This used the nameplates previously carried by 09008 and still lacked the requisite apostrophe! Six months later, 08879 stands outside the depot on 5 October, the yellow ends being highly unusual in lacking the normally de rigueur black wasp stripes.

The Rotherham scrapyard of C. F. Booth has processed many shunters over the years, with numerous Class 08s arriving during the fleet reduction of the early 1990s. On 26 March 1994, an anonymous 08671 awaits the cutting torch, having been withdrawn from Gateshead in November 1988. Alongside is 08296, a shunter which would become noteworthy for swapping identities with 08787 while withdrawn at Crewe Works in 1992, leading to much confusion and a legacy today of 08787 still operating as 08296 with Mendip Rail.

Overhauled in July 1989, 08824 was given Railfreight triple grey with General cabside repeaters, becoming one of only four Class 08s to feature this rarely used sub-sector branding on the livery. On an unrecorded date, 08824 is seen out of service and with its coupling rods removed at RFS' original maintenance site at Kilnhurst, near Rotherham, but it would survive the experience to work for another two decades.

The open day at Doncaster Works on 12 July 1992 provided an opportunity to see works pilot 08647 *Crimpsall* up close, still carrying the LNER apple green livery applied in May 1989. Unexpectedly, the loco was withdrawn in April 1993 and initially stored at Doncaster Carr and then Crewe Works. During 1997, it was sold to Harry Needle and taken to the South Yorkshire Railway, but only for breaking up for spares.

By the time of the next Doncaster Works open weekend on 9–10 July 1994, a new dedicated pilot had been installed in the form of 08682. Repainted in a fresh coat of BR blue, it was named *Lionheart* during the event to mark the 800th anniversary of the granting of the first royal charter to the town by King Richard I.

With Doncaster Works having passed into private ownership the previous year, the BRML logos carried by 08682 had given way to ABB ones when the shunter was recorded in Doncaster West Yard on 15 October 1996, shunting new Class 365 'Networker Express' unit 365538. Following the closure of Doncaster Works, 08682 would be relocated to Derby Litchurch Lane, where it remained until 2020 when sold to Harry Needle.

When not out on hire, RFS' fleet of Class 08s could normally be found at Doncaster. 08764 had been withdrawn with minor collision damage in May 1988, being immediately sold to RFS and duly repaired, becoming 003 *Florence*. On 30 October 1993, the shunter had not long returned from working Channel Tunnel construction trains at Cheriton, the '96' on its bonnet door being its identity while based there.

Also on 30 October 1993, 002 *Prudence*, better known as 08164, was in use as works pilot at Doncaster, shunting a newly overhauled Shell TEA tanker. This was another former Gateshead loco that had been acquired in 1988 following withdrawal in March 1986. As it was vacuum-braked only, it was mostly used in this role until sold into preservation at the East Lancashire Railway in 1998, where it remains.

Such was the demand for Class 08s for use on Channel Tunnel construction trains, RFS reached agreement with BR to sub-hire a considerable number of additional locos. These came from several depots, including March and Stratford, with 08713 seen at Doncaster Carr on 26 March 1994. Still carrying its hire number of RS073, it had spent much of 1993 at Cheriton. The hire work could be demanding though, and several BR machines suffered mechanical or electrical damage that ended their careers.

March 1990 saw 08500 transformed into a striking all-red livery at York, where it served as pilot for the wagon repair shops. By 8 May 1993, the loco was newly arrived at Doncaster Carr, having spent the previous two years based at Knottingley. The livery was largely still as initially applied with unofficial *Thomas* name, General cabside repeaters and York Clifton logos, but the number '1' was gone from below the name.

Prior to an appearance at the Worksop open day in September 1993, 08500 was given a spruce up, the most obvious change being the replacement of the General repeater stripes with Coal ones. The depot logos were additionally removed from the cabsides and the missing '1' reinstated on the other side. By 3 December 1994, a now grubby 08500 was back at Doncaster and under Loadhaul ownership.

While some Class 08s spent decades at one depot, others were more nomadic. By the time 08813 was recorded at Doncaster Carr on 29 March 1994, its homes had included Tyseley, Bescot, Tinsley, Finsbury Park, Bounds Green and Stratford, while the loco had also survived a withdrawal attempt in 1981. Repainted in Departmental grey in May 1991, it was stored by EWS in January 2000, but a further 11 years would pass before it was scrapped.

Released from Kilnhurst less than two months earlier, 09005 was stabled at Knottingley on 3 May 1992, in the company of 47550. The shunter had moved north from the Southern Region the previous autumn, with one of its new jobs in West Yorkshire being to trip HAA coal hoppers between Milford Sidings and Knottingley for maintenance and return repaired examples. It would later gain small Railfreight Coal logos.

The dedicated parcels platforms at Leeds station provided employment for a Neville Hill Class 08 into the early 1990s, with 08908 recorded on duty in September 1991 as it marshals Mk.1 BGs and GUVs. The shunter had arrived in the city in August 1987, going on to become part of the Midland Mainline fleet upon privatisation under the company's Maintrain division. It is still at Neville Hill today.

Holbeck lost its shunter allocation early in 1990, being reduced to a stabling point thereafter for locos working around Hunslet Yard and Stourton. 08581 had arrived at Neville Hill from Motherwell in June 1992 and was still carrying its former depot's salmon emblem when recorded at Holbeck on 14 June the following year. It would soon move on to Tinsley and then Doncaster, with storage coming in 1995 and disposal in 2000.

Under InterCity, Neville Hill was responsible for maintaining HST sets employed on three routes, so it was no great surprise to see 08950 repainted into the sector's colours in April 1993, this being the InterCity Mainline variant albeit with a swallow emblem. Named *Neville Hill 1st* at the same time, the shunter is seen at the depot two months later on 20 June. As well as a drophead buckeye, a pocket fitted alongside the front steps also allows a bar coupling to be carried for attaching to the nose end of HST power cars.

Knottingley's 08782 was handed a prestigious task on 21 October 1993, when it was charged with transferring the prototype English Electric Deltic to the National Railway Museum. This was newly arrived in York following its extraction from the Science Museum in London and transfer north by road. Unloading took place at ABB's York Works, with the short-distance rail trip completing the long-planned operation.

Only one Class 08 was graced with Railfreight Petroleum sub-sector emblems and then only the cabside repeaters, 08388 being recorded at its home depot of Immingham in July 1991. It did receive the appropriate 'scroll and star' depot plaques though, these being partially applied over the data panel. Although stored in August 1996, it was not scrapped until September 2010 after a decade stored on an industrial estate in Newton Heath, Manchester, in a failed preservation attempt.

The wonderfully named Botanic Gardens depot in Hull ceased to carry out significant maintenance activities in 1987, being reduced to a fuelling and stabling point thereafter. During 1992, the operational Railfreight triple grey duo of 08418 and 08525 stand inside the depot building, with withdrawn 08777 and 08308 behind. 08777 had been withdrawn in November 1991, while 08308 was laid up in February 1992.

Class 08s sold into industrial use could be found at work on Humberside during the early 1990s, including RFS-owned 08331. This had been acquired by the company in April 1988 following its withdrawal from Doncaster Carr the previous month, duly taking on the identity of 001 *Terence*. On 14 September 1993, it was recorded at Flixborough Wharf, to the west of Scunthorpe, where export steel traffic was handled.

Following withdrawal in October 1990, 08871 was sold to Humberside Sea and Land Services and transferred from Immingham to Grimsby Docks two months later. By 4 September 1993, it was anonymous in a light blue livery and also in use on steel traffic. It remained largely forgotten until 2001, when it was acquired by Cotswold Rail and then RMS Locotec six years later, where it remains part of the hire fleet today.

08575 displays both of Thornaby's trademarks while stabled at the Teesside depot on 31 March 1990, these being the customised paintwork and kingfisher emblem. The shunter had transferred to the depot from Gateshead in January 1986 and would remain until November 1992, when it moved on to Neville Hill. It would become part of the Freightliner fleet upon privatisation, but was stored in 2010 after incurring damage in a shunting incident at Southampton. 13 years later, it was stored at Nemesis Rail's Burton depot as a spares donor.

08931's career was over as it resides in store at Thornaby on 18 August 1996, now in EWS ownership, although it had been stopped the previous summer while owned by Loadhaul. The repeated number on the exhauster cabinet had been acquired while still in traffic, but the Regional Railways lettering on the battery box was seemingly added after it was stood down, the loco never belonging to the sector.

More industrial Class 08s could be found on Teesside with 08502 and 08503 located at ICI's Wilton works on 4 February 1995. Both had been acquired by the chemical giant in 1988, being officially withdrawn from BR stock that autumn after arriving at Wilton. The duo had been repainted by 1995 and carried both ICI and Railfreight Distribution logos with 08502, nearest the camera, also bestowed with a Thornaby kingfisher.

Slightly further west, AV Dawson had acquired 08774 from BR in September 1988 after initially hiring it from Thornaby over that summer. Based at the company's Middlesbrough terminal, the shunter is seen in April 1990, having gained a red livery and the name *Arthur Vernon Dawson*. The loco is still employed by AV Dawson today and, as the firm's operations have grown, it has been joined by three sister shunters.

Despite the distance involved, the shunter for Sunderland South Dock came from the Blyth Cambois allocation in the early 1990s rather than Gateshead or Heaton upon the former's closure. Overhauled at Crewe Works in February 1989, 08442 was stabled for the weekend amid a sea of Type 5 power on 3 May 1992. It had transferred to Blyth in April 1989, moving on to Doncaster in November 1992.

The Class 08s based at Gateshead came under the sponsorship of the Parcels sector for a time in 1990–91, this being justification enough to re-livery three of the fleet in a variation of the sector's new red and grey livery. During February 1992, 08888 *Postman's Pride* occupies the usual position for the Newcastle station pilot, its repaint having taken place the previous April. 08578 *Libert Dickinson* had been the first to gain Parcels colours in October 1990, while 08701 *Gateshead TMD 1852-1991* was the third and last in July 1991.

# Chapter 5
# Anglia Region

At the beginning of the 1990s, Stratford had one of the largest Class 08 allocations of all, with around 40 examples on its books. This was no great surprise given the area covered, which stretched from the already mentioned southern end of the East Coast Main Line through to the Suffolk coast. In East London, the duties included Temple Mills, Dagenham, Ripple Lane, Bow freight depot, Leyton engineers' yard, Purfleet and the carriage sidings at Thornton Fields. Also on the roster were the Freightliner terminals at Tilbury and Stratford, Ilford depot and Shell's Thames Haven refinery. With Colchester's shunter allocation now abolished, Stratford provided two Class 08s here, three at Harwich and five or six around Ipswich, with the occasional hire to Felixstowe for its container terminal.

Norwich Class 08s now just worked locally, following the withdrawal of other duties at the likes of Lowestoft and Great Yarmouth, which typically meant depot pilot duties at Crown Point and a station shunter. Cambridge's allocation also stayed largely local, with one out-based at Bury St Edmunds engineers' yard and another closer to home at Chesterton Junction. Lastly, the small March allocation also extended out to King's Lynn and Peterborough.

With the coming of privatisation, Trainload Freight South East took charge of a much smaller Stratford fleet as duties across the region contracted substantially. Elsewhere, Ilford gained two shunters to call its own, while the Anglia train operating unit had three Norwich Class 08s assigned to it. The Cambridge allocation passed to Rail Express Systems, while the closure of March in the spring of 1994 saw its allocation abolished.

**Allocated to Stratford in March 1989, 08498 was one of the depot's shunters selected to work at Cheriton on Channel Tunnel construction trains, gaining the hire number of RS074 on the fuel tank. Dispatched to Kent in September 1992, it did not survive the experience and was withdrawn in January 1994. Two months later, it was recorded at Stratford on 19 March, about to be scrapped on site by the Bird Group. Notably, the loco has been plastered with modern yellow and white overhead electrification warnings along the cantrail and by the cab door, four years before they became standard on UK locos, as an international workforce would not necessarily understand BR's own warning notices.**

Stratford was clearly ready for winter on 8 December 1991, as 08909 stands on the depot sandwiched between two Beilhack snowploughs. Converted from redundant Class 40 bogies, ADB965579 became well known for its painted shark's mouth. The shunter remained based in East London until 1997.

The previous Class 08 in Great Eastern Railway blue, 08833, had been converted to 09101 in the summer of 1992, bringing the demise of the livery. Colchester revived the look in November 1993 by repainting Stratford-based 08593 in a similar fashion, restoring its original D3760 number and adding a painted *Colchester TMD* name. The shunter is seen inside the small depot building upon completion.

08767 was just four months from withdrawal as it basks in the autumn sunshine at Parkeston Quay, Harwich, on 3 October 1993. With the abolition of Colchester's shunter allocation, Harwich pilots were now provided by Stratford as was the rest of Suffolk and Essex. Stood down on 31 January 1994, it was sold relatively quickly to the North Norfolk Railway, where it still enjoys retirement.

Before the staff at Colchester got around to 08593, they had already repainted two of its Stratford classmates into Departmental grey back in June 1993. Both received embellishments, with 08414 gaining the name *Whyte Wharf* and small Railfreight Distribution logos. In contrast, the pictured 08689 received much larger Railfreight General brandings and the name *Gateway to Europe*. Appropriately enough, it was on duty at Parkeston Quay a year later on 26 June 1994.

With its connecting rods decorated with wasp stripes, 08526 rests next to the fuelling point at Ipswich stabling point on an unrecorded date in the early 1990s. This was another duty now resourced by Stratford, where the shunter was based between 1991–96. Ipswich was always a good bet to see a Class 08 in action throughout the decade, and Freightliner still has examples of the class based at its maintenance depot in 2023.

Stratford clearly did not mind Colchester stealing its thunder as the depot struck once more in August 1992 by outshopping the only Class 08 ever to carry the grey and yellow Civil Engineers 'Dutch' colour scheme. 08752 is seen at work in Ipswich shortly after completion and also carrying the name *Suffolk Punch* on the cabsides with accompanying horse motif. The livery would be retained until 2002 when EWS was applied.

Norwich Crown Point adopted 08869 as its depot 'pet', outshopping it in green in May 1987 and naming it *The Canary* after the nickname of the city's football club. The celebrity shunter is seen on the depot during the summer of 1990 and it would pass to what would become Anglia Railways with privatisation. However, it suffered fire damage in the autumn of 1997 and never worked again, scrapping finally taking place in January 2011.

For a time, 08538 and 08540 seemed to be inseparable, transferring from March to Cambridge together in January 1988, back to March in July 1990 and then to Toton in March 1994 with Trainload Freight South East. In August 1993, the pair were stabled together by the fuelling point at March. Both were also overhauled in 1991 but as the cab paintwork demonstrates, 08538 was done at Crewe and 08540 at Kilnhurst.

The tradition of March depot accumulating withdrawn locos was still in evidence on 28 December 1992, as 08889 heads a line up of redundant Class 08s that also features 08936, 08859, 08868 and Network SouthEast-liveried 08631. All but 08889 had been condemned that month, the odd loco out having gone in March that year. Remarkably, the trio of 08631, 08868 and 08936 would all survive and still exist in 2023.

08865 was stopped for engine repairs at Cambridge on 6 August 1994, now coming under the Rail Express Systems banner. The shunter had arrived at the depot in January 1988 after a period in store at Derby Locomotive Works and would remain in East Anglia for almost a decade. Inevitably, it would become an EWS machine and then pass to HNRC ownership in 2015, serving today in the company's hire fleet.

Another Class 08 to move to Cambridge at the start of 1988 was 08539, which is seen on top of the depot fuel tanks during 1991. This one failed to make it to Rail Express Systems ownership, being condemned in March 1992 while owned by Railfreight Distribution. The following year saw it stripped for parts at Crewe Works, after which it was moved to MC Metals at Glasgow and broken up in October 1993.

The second Class 08 to gain RES red/grey was 08757, which was painted at Cambridge in September 1993 and gained the *Eagle CURC* nameplates previously carried by 08631 at the same time. On 6 August 1994, it was stabled atop parcels vans near the depot, but would lose the nameplates a year later upon transfer to Heaton. It still carries the livery today in preservation at the Telford Steam Railway.

# Chapter 6
# Scottish Region

For the ever-decreasing number of shunters based in Scotland, the earliest years of the 1990s were marked by a period of reorganisation and consolidation. This was most notable at Eastfield, the Glasgow depot beginning the decade with no shunters officially allocated there, despite its considerable fleet of main line locos. This changed in August 1991 with the mass migration of Haymarket's Class 08s to the other end of the Edinburgh–Glasgow main line. The same month also saw Eastfield take on the three Class 08s still officially allocated to Thornton Junction and the two Glasgow Works pilots. Thereafter, the depot supplied shunters back to all three locations and also sent them to Craigentinny, Millerhill, Perth, Polmadie, Coatbridge Freightliner terminal and Waverley station.

On the other side of Glasgow, Motherwell's allocation still covered the depot's carriage and wagon shops and also held sway at Mossend Yard, British Steel Ravenscraig and Fort William. Slightly surprisingly, Grangemouth depot still had an allocation of just two Class 08s, one to work around the docks and freight terminals while the other was held in reserve.

Away from the Central Belt, just a handful of shunters could be found by 1992. Ayr's small fleet covered the nearby Falkland Yard and Stranraer, for example, while Aberdeen's three Class 08s shared two duties and the same was true at Inverness.

The impending closure of Eastfield saw its shunters moved across Glasgow to Motherwell in August 1992 and these duly passed to Transrail control, as did the Ayr Class 08s. The Aberdeen allocation was similarly done away with in July 1993 and subsequently became an out-based duty from Motherwell. With the preparations for privatisation, Glasgow Works gained two Class 08s back again in March 1994, while Inverness had a pair assigned for ScotRail operations. Similarly, Craigentinny was also allocated a brace of shunters for the East Coast train operating unit.

**Three 'shunters' that were rarely pictured or reported were 97601–03, which were converted at Kilmarnock in 1986 from the power units of scrapped ballast cleaners for use as depot shunters. While they spent long periods out of use, 97603 eventually found a home based at Dalmeny to work a dedicated maintenance train on the Forth Bridge. 97601 was employed in a similar role at Dundee to cover the Tay Bridge while 97602 was based at the Civil Engineers workshops at Kilmarnock. All three were also notable for being incorrectly numbered, carrying 97701–03. On 19 July 1996, 97603 stands at Dalmeny with the Forth Bridge maintenance train.**

One of the roles assigned to the Haymarket Class 08s was station pilot at Edinburgh Waverley, where they handled the Motorail traffic in particular. On 10 March 1990, InterCity Mainline-liveried 08570 was on duty, having gained its colours in August 1988. Although it made the move to Eastfield in August 1991, it was withdrawn at the start of the following year and cut up on site at Motherwell in September 1993.

Occupying a similar position and on the same duty at Waverley on 11 August 1991 was another of Haymarket's specially-liveried Class 08s, in the form of LNER green 08793. Painted back in July 1988, it was now rather scruffy and faded. The author has fond childhood memories of this loco shunting the Motorail vans containing the family car on a holiday to Scotland almost exactly a year earlier, in August 1990!

Provincial-liveried 08761 is seen stabled at Thornton Yard in September 1990 with CAR brake van B954852. The shunter had moved to Thornton from Haymarket three months earlier but the closure of the Speedlink wagonload network the following summer severely impacted the area's freight traffic. As a result, Thornton lost its shunter allocation in August 1991 with 08761 moving to Eastfield, withdrawal coming seven months later.

New to Ebbw Junction in September 1962, 08952 swapped Wales for Scotland in June 1975 with transfer to Eastfield, where it largely remained based for 12 years until moving to Motherwell. On 6 May 1991, it was residing on the latter depot but still carrying the West Highland terrier emblem of Eastfield. Yellow bufferbeams were unusual on a Class 08 by this date, as were the BR arrows on the battery box cover.

While stopped for repairs at Glasgow Works in the spring of 1993, Motherwell-based 08883 received a fresh coat of BR blue, emerging without double arrows. This led to erroneous reports in the railway magazines of the time that it had received Caledonian blue, which was not the case. Pictured on 10 April, the shunter is awaiting the return of its leading wheelset with the lifting eyes remaining in place on the bufferbeam.

By October 1990, Motherwell was responsible for providing the Class 08 out-based at Fort William, where RETB signalling-equipped 08853 was a long-term resident. Its duties included undertaking trip workings to the British Alcan aluminium smelter and Corpach paper mill, shunting the BP oil sidings and small yard, and acting as station pilot. It was on the latter job on this occasion, stabled atop the sleeper and Motorail stock.

Ayr's Class 08 allocation was rather isolated in the south west corner of Scotland and tended to go rather unnoticed. Even when the depot repainted some of its shunters in Railfreight triple grey, this did not always get reported. 08727 was one such machine and is seen in May 1992 with the white BR arrows on the battery box only just visible against the Rail grey. It would be withdrawn and scrapped the following year.

For a time, the three Class 08s based at Aberdeen were 08855, 08882 and LNER green-liveried 08793, with all three recorded together in Clayhills carriage sidings on 3 April 1994. However, both 08793 and 08855 had been condemned in July 1993, while 08882 had become part of the Motherwell allocation at the same time but remained out-based. Another two years would elapse before the withdrawn duo were moved away.

One of the reasons that the Aberdeen Class 08s could be down-sized was the arrival of the final Class 09/2 conversion in the city. 09205 had been allocated to Motherwell upon completion in December 1992 and moved to Aberdeen in July 1993 as its predecessors were condemned. On 3 April 1994, the former 08620 was recorded stabled in Guild Street sidings, from where it undertook trip workings to several locations.

The ScotRail train operating unit was assigned two Class 08s at Inverness upon its creation in March 1994; 08754 and, pictured here, 08762. These not only handled the soon to cease ScotRail loco-hauled formations but also marshalled the sleeper and Motorail stock upon its arrival from London each morning and then again in the evening. In July 1994, the debranded Class 08 shunts the car-carrying Mk.1 GUVs into position.

# Other books you might like:

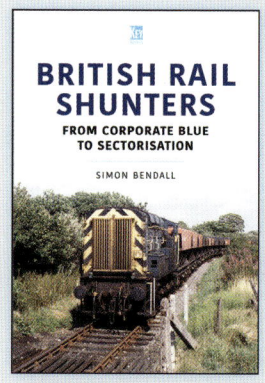

**BRITISH RAIL SHUNTERS**
FROM CORPORATE BLUE TO SECTORISATION
SIMON BENDALL

Britain's Railways Series, Vol. 46

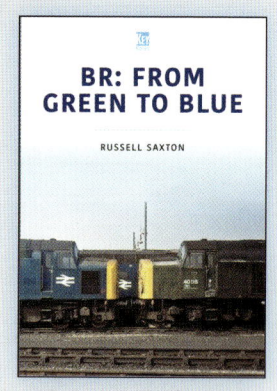

**BR: FROM GREEN TO BLUE**
RUSSELL SAXTON

Britain's Railways Series, Vol. 4

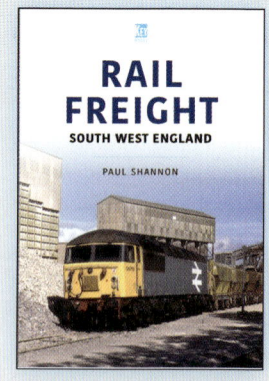

**RAIL FREIGHT**
SOUTH WEST ENGLAND
PAUL SHANNON

Railways and Industry Series, Vol. 5

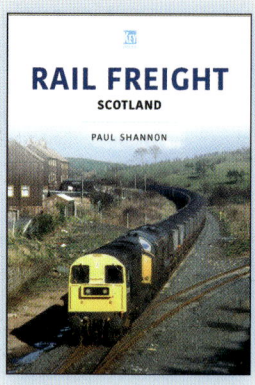

**RAIL FREIGHT**
SCOTLAND
PAUL SHANNON

Railways and Industry Series, Vol. 6

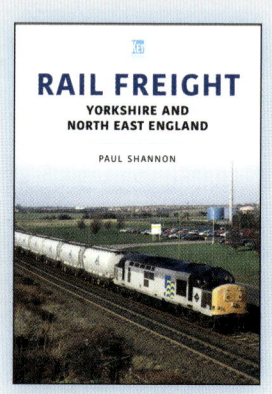

**RAIL FREIGHT**
YORKSHIRE AND NORTH EAST ENGLAND
PAUL SHANNON

Railways and Industry Series, Vol. 7

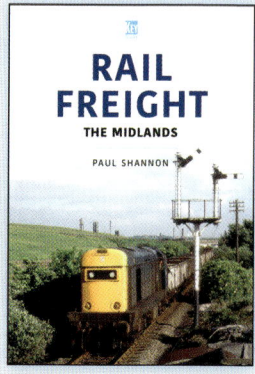

**RAIL FREIGHT**
THE MIDLANDS
PAUL SHANNON

Railways and Industry Series, Vol. 8

For our full range of titles please visit:
**shop.keypublishing.com/books**

# VIP Book Club

## Sign up today and receive
## TWO FREE E-BOOKS

Be the first to find out about our forthcoming book releases and receive exclusive offers.

Register now at **keypublishing.com/vip-book-club**

Our VIP Book Club is a 100% spam-free zone, and we will never share your email with anyone else. You can read our full privacy policy at: privacy.keypublishing.com